Of Symbols Misused

Mary-Jane Newton

Proverse Hong Kong

Man, according to Kenneth Burke, is 'the symbol-using (symbol-making, symbol-mis-using) animal … separated from his natural condition by instruments of his own making'.[1] It is a preoccupation with this making, with the fruits of this (mis-)using and with the nature of the separation that they incur, that animates Mary-Jane Newton's first collection of poetry. Much of the variety in **OF SYMBOLS MISUSED** is touched by man's existential dilemma as a self-conscious being obliged to live his sunniest moments in the shadow of death and construct meaning in the maw of absurdity. Engaging with this dilemma, Newton shows an exultance with words and a commitment to exploring the elucidations and complications engendered by words as the primary tools of man's sometimes puny, sometimes magnificent, efforts to tell a story about himself.

MARY-JANE NEWTON was born in Goa in 1983, and spent the first years of her life in India. She subsequently grew up in Germany and England, and now grows up in Hong Kong. Mary-Jane's work has been published in literary journals and anthologies in Asia. 'Of Symbols Misused' is her first collection of poetry. She regularly reads at live poetry events in Hong Kong. With a background in linguistics, communication and cultural studies, Mary-Jane aims always to meet her reader elsewhere, other than where words command us: beyond and beneath their meanings.

Of Symbols Misused

Mary-Jane Newton

Proverse Hong Kong

Of Symbols Misused

Of Symbols Misused
by Mary-Jane Newton, 9 March 2011.
Copyright © Proverse Hong Kong, 9 March 2011.

Second edition published in Hong Kong by Proverse Hong Kong,
5 July 2020.
ISBN-13: 978-988-8492-05-3

1st published in Hong Kong by Proverse Hong Kong, 9 March 2011.
ISBN: 978-988-19321-5-0

Enquiries to: Proverse Hong Kong, P.O. Box 259, Tung Chung Post
Office, Tung Chung, Lantau, NT, Hong Kong, SAR.
Web: http://www.proversepublishing.com

Cover design by Grace Chan.

Proverse Hong Kong

British Library Cataloguing in Publication Data (for 1st edition)

Newton, Mary-Jane.
Of symbols misused.
I. Title II. Bickley, Gillian
821.9'2-dc22

ISBN-13: 9789881932150

Author's Acknowledgments

First and foremost, I'd like to thank my husband, Toby Newton, for his continuous support and encouragement. I am much obliged to the knowledgeable and experienced editors at Proverse Hong Kong whose help in shaping this volume was indispensable. My thanks also to Peter Carpenter who wrote the Preface. Grace Chan has created the cover with a fine eye to detail; my sincerest thanks to her. Many thanks to the following editors and writers who took the time to read and comment on this book: Martin Alexander, Gillian Bickley, Geoffrey Gatza, Michael Holland and Eddie Tay. Finally, I thank all poets of the Poetry OutLoud group in Hong Kong, who have served as muses and sounding boards.

PETER CARPENTER, who contributed the Preface to "Of Symbols Misused" has been a teacher of English and Creative Writing since 1980. He has been a Visiting Fellow at the University of Warwick since 1990 and was Creative Writing Fellow at the University of Reading during 2007–08. He was named a 'Poetry Teacher Trailblazer' by the Poetry Society, United Kingdom, where he is also a trustee and most recently was elected Chair. He has published five collections of poetry; *After the Goldrush* the latest, highly praised in the *Times Literary Supplement* and *Poetry London*; he is a co-director of Worple Press and a regular essayist and reviewer for a number of journals including *The Use of English* and *London Magazine*. He has been asked to write the chapter on Creative Writing for the forthcoming Oxford University Press *Handbook of Contemporary British and Irish Poetry*.

Of Symbols Misused

Preface

Mary-Jane Newton's first collection displays boldness of spirit and a buccaneering sense of adventure in its forays with language, matched by energy, a wry sense of humour and humility in the light of the poet's responsibilities, thus making it a joy to read, at turns sensuous and arch in tones and angles. Whether she is writing love poems, elegiac pieces, imagist fragments or poems that have a pondering of the slipperiness of language at their very heart, Newton's writing is distinguished by a mode of address that is 'simple, sensuous and passionate' to re-cast Milton's words.

She also displays a control and skill in the shaping of her material that is a promising sign for the continuing nourishment of her poetic voice. I say 'voice' but she has many voices and tones, refreshingly working around the trapdoor of a 'full on' confessional 'I'. The poet, W. H. Auden defined poetry as 'memorable speech' and there is much from this collection that sticks in the mind and rewards further readings. Sometimes the effects are subtly beautiful, as in 'Snowflake' where human apprehensions are shaped in the delicate falls and turns of short lines, with puns on lightness and dark enhanced by echoes of distant rhymes ('lightly...me'), carefully-managed enjambment ('and brush away//the sky...') and simplicity of diction:

> *I used to fall easily and lightly*
> *and glow in the dark.*

Now, I am a blizzard –
I want to break into smithereens
and brush away

the sky from which I fell
and the dark that surrounded me.

This brought to mind Blake's 'The Fly' – not a bad point of reference. The sequence 'Ten' which depends upon fluttering short lines and near rhymes for its impact summoned Pound and William Carlos Williams into the mental locker. In fact the impact of the whole collection is condensed in the last two lines of this: 'I dare you: /dance with me!' There are other echoes as well: Holub for example, in the ranging from a particular instance of experience towards some profound universal implication.

Newton is also skilled at fixing her poems in places and then inhabiting them with figures whose fractured narratives intrigue and ring true. Take the end of 'Better Than Before' where the urban landscape turns Hopper into Hitchcock via the 'dirty motels' that the unnamed and spooky male persona walks past before encountering his 'brown-haired lady':

I know her heel so well,
the way it nestles
in her stiletto. Tonight I shall
slit her throat with care;
and make sure her dress fits
better than before.

Again, here, it is Newton's control and detachment (the half rhymes of 'care' and 'before'; the trail in sound through 'it...stiletto...slit...fits') that intrigue and disturb.

Behind these poems we are always aware of an abiding intelligence; and the notes and citations in themselves indicate a scholarship that fortunately does not stifle or inhibit Newton's range. It is to her great credit that the poems which debate the limits of language are very often the ones that are simultaneously the most strident and off-beat. I loved 'The Toecutter' and 'Contemplations' for example; both have a clarity, playfulness and wit that sidestep sententiousness.

That Newton pulls it off again and again throughout the collection is a great sign for the future: her boldness and craft are sufficient to carry the big ideas to her readers via concrete and resonant images, as at the end of the evocative and sensuous 'The Snowberry in Me':

This phlegmatic solitude defines the I.
Your love is my frost.
I carry your winter within me.

Peter Carpenter
Tonbridge, July 2010

Of Symbols Misused

For Douglas, the cat
and Toby, my favourite human

Man is

the symbol-using (symbol-making, symbol-misusing)
animal
inventor of the negative (or moralized by the negative)
separated from his natural condition by instruments of his
own making
goaded by the spirit of hierarchy (or moved by the sense
of order)
and rotten with perfection.

Kenneth Burke

Table of Contents

I   Doors and Traps

II   A Conch to Save

III Ten

IV The Open Window

Of Symbols Misused

Of Symbols Misused

I

Doors and Traps

Of Symbols Misused

If You Are a Poet

If you are a poet, kneel!

If you are a poet, wash your hands with oil.
Throttle the king;
love better the weak;
turn a blind and hungry eye.

If you are a poet, paint the dove white.
Spit in the yawn of my face.
Swallow the needles;
whisper to the Gods.

If you are a poet, bleed out;
forget the red silken band.
Watch the lazy clock;
miss the train.

If you are a poet, deny!

If you are a poet, sleep in the warmth of my lap.
Throw the piano;
bend the unbendable;
send back the message.

If you are a poet, sink in the shallow water;
slap your aching wrists;
look up to the liars;
smell the burnt air.

Of Symbols Misused

If you are a poet, shuffle the cards;
fly, fly like a drunken goose;
bury the treasure;
hold shut your heart.

If you are a poet, leave!

If you are a poet, return to your body.
Study the curved breast.
Lick the dry sand from your lips;
smile at the jester.

If you are a poet, draw longer your brow.
Plunge deeper the dagger;
lose your temper;
follow the wild stallion.

If you are a poet, take the blame:
march on the barren fields,
set free the broken birds,
lie still in your pain.

If you are a poet, wane with the moon!

If you are a poet, tie me to the mast.
Meet me half way,
drink the full cup,
set fire

to your

weary
body.

To Peter Weiss[2]
or *Albert Blades*

Here in my confinement, extinguished lights
draw close the coat of night insects, which brings
to me the loss of things I barely possessed.
You know, your absence weighs heavy — adds
years on top of those that I count mine.

This dark here may or may not concertina time:
I observe the sea of glow-worms spiralling still,
spiralling clearly and ever more beautifully into
the proximity ... the distance ... the proximity
again. After all, memories, like moths,

are drawn unto the very flame that burns
their wings. I feel my fever's heat failing this
moment, so full of expectation, no longer stripping bare
the walls. I see you lift yourself, drooping, hairy dusk;
I imagine another radiance awaits you.

I would prefer things darker in my cage, and so too
the vermin. But my years unfold me now, they unfurl me
like an old, ragged banner whose long arm reaches out to
the horizon behind these dark and angry bars —
and so I watch it flutter gaily now, downwind.

Chess

A Love Poem

'Peel it all away,' I said to the pawn
who made this move and that,
'To get to me,' I added.
Sheepishly, I looked down onto
the white square that bore my feet.
It was those fantasies of
an aristocratic life that turned me
naked. A laughing stock.

'And by the way, I love you.'
A roosting bird fell from its pole.
You moved to black. You drew from
your limbs an ace of hearts;
cornered my queen.
A sigh. Was it yours? Or mine?
Uncertain, I falter. The verb
'To give' is forbidden in this game,

that isn't really a game. We know
that much. 'I apologize,' I said,
and mean it. But I dare you;
juxtapose a sickness after love!

My shame fades my desire.
The last move dawns.

Goodbye

Now that you are gone
I can feel
the scent of your hair on my skin.
O I can feel
your breath moving the hair on my neck;

your eyes on mine;
your wrist by my heart.

Swollen with blood
it will turn black and burst.
Cry your tears of good-bye,
like dark berries rolling
over your beautiful cheeks!

Near to your lungs
is where I want to be again!

Old Lovers

We are old lovers now.
Like rancid butter we drip
all over the sheets.
We smile at
the mutiny of our bodies
and we lie, holding hands.
We know we both
remember the full moons
during which we chased
our scents like unruly hounds,
during which we burnt
ourselves up like cheap candles,
during which we played gently
each other like instruments,
read each other like Braille,
watched each other
with closed eyes.
Now we lie here,
at once regretful and reconciled,
holding hands
under the duvet.

Cardiac Arrest

The red bird soars again.
Like a gurgling electric current
life returns and awareness
resettles in my breath.
Stronger wings flutter;
the drooping head perks.
A doctor's glassy eyes
fall from dire grey
like black pellets
pressed in thin crust.

A rigid blackness withers.
My red bird wakens, unstops its beak,
and stretches waxen wings
to recall endless exertion,
a nauseating strain aimed at
blackness as heavy as a full stop.
My bird's frail body folded up
into a tiny box of steel:
Houdini[3] trapped,
trembling in stupor.

Mighty red bird — are you
origami or papier mâché? —
your wings are dipped in tar.
A male medic, a female:
'Work with us!'
The faintest chirrup, the feeblest twitter,
lack of sensation
as a needle pierces my arm.
Thump. The stretcher.
A golden cage, bearing a lost feather.

And suddenly:
the vital pain of fists on my chest,
pale gasps of party guests
like ripples deep under the surface
that is our usual life, the flight of birds.

Air makes it worse, grips my chest,
fades the boat
my feet connect to;
the red bird chokes mid-song.

Air
The urge for
Air

First there is sickness.
My bird topples.
I talk to guests,
enjoy myself, while
the red bird draws
large circles.

Guilt and Blame

Your white and lonely face,
like soaring cherry blossoms,
faded in a sad wind's breath.
You left in the dark, without your shoes;
a red robe sailing the night,
a midnight moon sailing the sky.

Come, come, little child,
don't cry. See how I, timidly,
kiss your hair and how your feet can
also touch the morning sky?
Not I but the snow now bears
your traces like proud scars.

I am the one to cry. For all, all
is lost now and this putrid blood marks
all our hands. It was you who,
unstained by others and their ways,
unhooked herself from
a course mapped out and undisputed.

Ah, little one, hear me plead:
Spare yourself for us. For guilt is heavier
than blame and you contain
your absence. Have mercy and return.
But I already see the grey in your steps
and the lightness that separates us.

Your white and lovely face,
like soaring cherry blossoms,
faded in a ...

Vaterland

Even your streets smell of you
and the summer cries your name,
Germany.

I was young
and foremost selfish
when I knew you.
You were my people's republic.

Now you linger like a steaming
bareness, unable to dry off,
Germany.

You are my realm of eagles
that never endured.
When I think of you,
you vanish like a compliment.

An empty register without names,
you remain open still,
Germany.

There are no blossoms here,
no heightened smell.
Without you,
everything is everywhere.

In you I set my vocabulary.
From you I uncouple.
Good-bye,
Germany.

Olymp is Us

You hurl your wit at me, off-the-cuff,
like mighty Zeus his lighting rods;
you carry me away on your winged words,
as only a booted Hermes does.

Not one of Athena's bravest soldiers could
bear the strain of this sweet battle;
an amused Ares rubs his hands together;
Artemis sends out her drooling hounds.

As strong and proud as Poseidon,
you burst my fundament; my pillars fall.
Like Hera, you govern me with virtue;
a mad Dionysus, you set a blaze in my thought.

Nyx won't hide me; Ananke snickers;
Chronos strokes his grey, age-old beard;
and Tartarus ... Tartarus pokes the deepest fire;
Hades licks his fingers, woe is me!

Moirae, I beg you, untie this knot!
See, I am no heroic myth!
No Titan lives within me.
My Trojan horse is not a ploy.

And Achilles watches me lose
this battle
of honesty.

The Lands of Ishmanoor

I am a raging sea
My blood to reach thy shore;
I am a whirling wind
To touch thy inner core.

My heart is like a golden shell
That to thee I've given;
My journey to the lands of Ishmanoor,
May it be forgiven.

I am a poison oak —
My roots reach out for thee;
I am a wild forgotten skull
Whose eyes no longer see.

The golden lands of Ishmanoor
That lie behind my frontal lobes —
There I sent my men of death
In flowing scarlet robes.

I am a mountain tall,
My foot is dark and wide.
I am a desert vast and dry;
No place for thee to hide.

I have loved thee deep and true,
The spark of youth a blast;
The fire lands of Ishmanoor
Are but a dead hand of the past.

You Me

Your salty ocean water in a nacre conch
My bitter-sweet tears in a wooden nutshell

Your diamond ice pick
My glass needle

The mist caught high in your banyan trees
The dust on the pages of my latest, unused diary

Your icy glacier clouds, the rhythm of eternity
My flowing waters, the tune of oblivion

Your cream-coloured safety net
My lush lilac cobweb

Your elegant parachute over a rainbow
My wet dandelion seed in an oily puddle

The laughing sunflower of your genius
The smiling seeds of my madness

Your angels, curly hair and silver lashes
My gals next door, aluminium halo and plastic
       fingernails

You Me

Tied together with the silky band of the Milky Way
Held apart by the marble bars of a volcanic epicentre

Separated
The cosmos:
These little heads of ours.

Seven Lies Speaking

Seeking refuge between the layers of your truth,
you will let us speak to you in our electric, sticky hums.

And you, you will let us sit between two lungs, embed us
       in your trenches,
where we'll swear to fight for you and where we'll leave
our bootless blood frozen in mid-beat. That is,
if you pay the ransom, as we are costly gifts to be
       received.

But you here? You will let us clutch your throat and
       reasoning;
and as for the latter, we will squat and bloat our thin and
brittle skins, until we pop like old party balloons
       forgotten in a corner.

Oh yes … and you! You, filled with desire and
       deficiency, will reach for us
with a pulse wet and eager. And we, your brides, will
       sway
for you and bend and twist and swerve your way, until
our swooning necks are thin as paper, dancing on our
       shoulders.

And you there, you will breathe onto our tempered shells
       to view the
bitter steam obscuring our scenery.

But what with you, I wonder? Who now, is the knife
and who now the bearer? And yes, you too.
You will let us be your cherished screws, and we will
       anchor you
in our patchworked skies, breaking from the middle.

Big Fish

Now, now little fool,
who dances
with the swordfish
and asks the sea horse
for a date,
practice moderation!
Ask the anemone first.
Practice getting closer,
without her shrinking.
Charm the blowfish.
Chaperone the
algae swaying with the
relentless current.
Remember, being a big fish
demands time
and patience,
and can never, never
be rushed.

Just a Shadow

Love is without pain:
She is blossom, she is bliss,
And through your body's every vein
You shall know my kiss.

Love is without wrath:
With love, there's always a tomorrow;
Let my love create a path
That to my heart you follow.

Love pledges without ending:
She is gentle, she is kind;
But truly, she is just pretending
Love's a shadow of the mind.

Denial of Death[4]

Oh yes
I have lived my poems;
have seen the fuller air,
the brighter sky,
even freer the freedom.

And yet,
it is all a perjury
at the highest court;
a cabled intrigue,
a false dewdrop's blight.

For my ferocity has been a shield.
My boldness? A crust.

Let us send
a glance back
to wave to the juggins
on this molehill
that is our world.

Satsumas and White Crockery

Then my mother entered.

Against the walls squatted an old child's
cradle with feet as tired as her own;
she moved towards it, crossing a room
furnished with satsumas and white crockery.
Dismayed, she wailed concerning a jigsaw
puzzle. As for the missing pieces, I knew

they were stashed behind a wooden door that
whispered upon opening. Taking seven steps
toward the door, I did not move. Then it dawned
on me, as clear as thunderclouds:

My mother wore my father's body, preaching
as she climbed upon a wooden pedestal:
Beauty is a splinter in the eye of the beholder.
Pain is an ocean in the body of the bearer.

Here I analyze a censored wish for safety,
before pain and beauty, before the
enormity of being pushed and dragged
by a midwife into daylight, as a poet of this world.
Then I saw her again, and her affection
withered at our awkward touch.

By now I flew with greatest labour
above Lord Black of Crossharbour,[5]
who, dressed in black, watched us caress,
a clock in hand. The ticking rose.
He tinkered round the edges of my sheets.

Of Symbols Misused

To him, I said:

Hand me the smallest canvas for
my secondary revision.[6]
I paint my mother entering
in the oranges and blues of
satsumas and white crockery ...

Snowflake

I used to fall easily and lightly
and glow in the dark.

Now, I am a blizzard —
I want to break into smithereens
and brush away

the sky from which I fell
and the dark that surrounded me.

Better Than Before

The sleepers of this tired city
see not the man I am, nor the
walk I take past
these dark forgotten alleyways.

Dirty motels watch me through
greasy unused curtains,
their lights, monotonously,
spill out to the city:
M-O-T-E-L, M-O-T-E-L,
M-O-T-E-L

Red shadows feel up a wet
glistening pavement
as I enter the house.
She is there,
my brown-haired lady.

I know her heel so well,
the way it nestles
in her stiletto. Tonight, I shall
slit her throat with care;
and make sure her dress fits
better than before.

II

A Conch to Save

Of Symbols Misused

Poor Beggar

I saw you on the street
begging for a penny;
I gave you my wallet.

I saw you on the street
begging for warmth;
I gave you my clothes.

I saw you on the street
begging for love;
I gave you my heart.

I saw you on the street
begging for more;
I cut off my fingers, pulled out my lashes;

I cut open my wrist,
gave you a bowl of warm blood;
gave you the dew of my breath;
gave you the music of my soul.

I saw you on the street
running;
your arms full,
your haul heavy.

I saw you turn around

and bend down
for one of my toes
that you had dropped on the way.
Run, poor beggar, run!
Never look back!

Never return!
For you left me prosperous,
light and free.

A London Winter

If
Of these many fallen petals
One to you seems fair,
So fair,
May winter-love blow snow and wind
Until
It settles on your hair!

May
The gods of richest wishes
Fill
Your eyes with joy and bliss,
And may they cast to you,
My love,
The angel's eager kiss!

No Metaphor

China, we dance today.
She is the forest's exhilarating bride,
she tears all with her tenderness.
When we turn our backs, she sighs
in the ocean's lungs.

China, we drink today;
to her plum blossoms that lay
in beds of the sweetest porcelain.
Bitter rice wine, fickle friends.

China, we hear
her sublime scream in the dark —
with her child-like nonchalance;
she has rendered all but one
combustible.

China, we once held each other steady
as I shook in her arms.

China, we gasp in our elementalism.
She is no play with futile words,
she is no sunken metaphor.

Paperdragons

Sometimes I hear them,
the paperdragons;
the way they sing
in small gentle voices,
accompanying the volcano.

There they sit,
surrounded by the spitting lava;
no trace of a flinch.
They sing of their lives
in small gentle voices.

Only a spark would suffice,
just a spark, a tiny spark.
But they don't know that.
They sing of their lives,

the paperdragons,
in small gentle voices
accompanying the volcano,
sitting amidst the spitting lava.

Wish

Follow the moon, the moon, the moon.
Follow the moon, follow the moon to peace.
I guess an unhappy mother makes an unhappy child.
Follow the moon, follow the moon to peace.

Follow the moon.
Follow the moon, like the sea follows the sands.
Back, forth, back, forth, back, forth, back, forth, back.
Follow the moon, like the sea follows the sands.

Follow the moon.
Follow the moon, follow the moon to love.
I guess two overcrowded *Is* make a lonely *We*.
Follow the moon, follow the moon to love.

Follow the moon.
Follow the moon, follow the moon home.
I guess a number of moons in a row makes a tunnel.
Follow the moon, follow the moon home.

Follow the moon.
Follow the moon, like the palms follow the sun.
Follow the moon, like the night follows the day.
Follow the moon, the moon, the moon.

Touching

Tonight, I touch. I hear your calling.
We slowly enter foreign grounds;
All masks and armour falling,
Hands following a scent like hounds.

We're melting outward, O so fast!
Each becoming part of what we touch.
The hourglass stands still at last.
Saying nothing, we say much.

The China tree is blooming often
We move at odds and yet together.
I can feel our edges blur. We soften
Become snow, and fur, and leather.

Hairclips caught in tangled sheets;
My fingers walk the gradient of your spine,
Counting bones like shifting beads;
Your thighs are moving against mine.

Flesh glides over bare flesh's heat.
I wonder: how long will we lie entwined?
Your heart is beating, your breath so deep.
We will find out in time.

Ode to My Husband

I commit to you,
in the belief that the years of love,
caring and intimacy
that we have shared together,
should be extended for the rest of our lives.

You read it
and so did I.

Let us celebrate all that which comes easily to us,
but seek also to overcome any future obstacles
that keep us from feeling safe and loved
in each other's hearts.

With a hot heart,
my breath icicled.

I commit to you,
and give you this ring as a token of this pledge.

And for a moment,
I trusted like a child again;
timeless and without concern.

Let us
repeat this moment
thousandfold,
to create the vessel
that is the rest of our lives.

Dear Sun

Dear sun,

A golden barque like you
I seek to sail —
adrift in a tight-spun cocoon.

I seek to repeat myself
in you and in your
permanent movement.

In your swaying hold
I seek transience.
Let me be unchanged.

III

Ten

Of Symbols Misused

I

Grass

You
pull
push
stroke
hit
talk
shout.

But the grass
does not grow
faster.

II

For You

This is a star for you.
Keep it cold and dry.
Wash inside out.
No bleach!

III

A Poet's Prerogative

Opening
your eyes
each morning
scorches off
the top layer
of the cells
on your retina.

Opening
your eyes
each morning
scorches off
an old you,
so you should see
the world with
new eyes.

IV

Homo Oniens

It is
as with
an onion:

There is
no core.

Its essence
is
its layers.

V

My Nylon Stocking[7]

New York
London

My nylon stocking
falls
at your feet.

Like two words
let's merge
into each other.

VI

Pullover

I tugged
just a little

and
it unraveled,

unwearable.

VII

To a Cog

You conceive yourself
larger than
the machine
that houses you.
This
will
be
your
downfall.

VIII

Stammer

The truth
came
spurting
in shots
of letters
like an old
telegraph:
I d-stop-d-stop-d-stop-
did.

IX

Epiphany

Where I thought
the mass to be,
I saw periphery.

The abyss was,
in fact, the edge;
the cloth mere seam;
the meat was vein.

And the land?
A border.

X

Dance

Sometimes
one step
is enough
to make the world
spin, whirl, swirl.

I dare you:
dance with me!

IV

The Open Window

Of Symbols Misused

Time Like a Dress

I have found you amidst
the scorched gravel
of my organs;
among the grey
remnants of my blood.
I have dug you up.

I gazed at you,
held you up to the light —
your silhouette
a warm white rose
across my face.
You were happenstance.

You harboured life:
it teemed.
When I was with you, I wore
time like a dress.
Where you fell,
I opened.

But you could not
bear my solitude;
like the Greek gods,
you became human.

Lover,
sooner or later,
everyone grows bored with
the beauty of a rose.

Coming of Age[8]

I

In the beginning,
the Earth entered the Sky
like a rusty screw.
Together, they turned and twisted,
and their union
brought forth the Light,
which begat the gamut of beings,
my people among them.

All were newly made,
still warm, membranous,
and steaming:
the mountains and the forests,
the elephant and his child, the turtle,
the snake and her child, the squid,
and all the creatures
of the heavens, sea and land.

In these swooning summer days,
our elders, clad in leather,
with magic hunting spears,
thanked the Gods
and roamed the vast plains
of this then fine land.

II

Now we drive, purposeful,
for roaming is inefficient.
We no longer thank the Gods
and the fertile days of our land,

we have spoilt with perfection.
Our Gods — look again —
have become daemons.
We have fashioned them

to our likeness.
Ugly are their heads and
many are their holy names.
Reason is the greatest
among them,
the ugliest and
the most tragic.
All corpses look the same
on an altar slain for money.

You, tribesman; hero!
On this stagnant summer day,
your rite of passage asks
you wrap your imagination
around you,
like a thick sheet of hide;
asks you keep warm
with intuition.

Kinsman,
gather the elephant and the snake.
Hold tight your magic spear.
Keep it safe for the battle.

Sediment

The lines of this poem
wind their way to
hug me — slick and glossy
snakes of poison.

There, it is done.
Their teeth have pierced
this neck they first caressed.
And what they bring

slowly amasses,
swells and bulges in
this tired sack of flesh,
and remains.

Scaled lengths of rope,
heads indistinguishable,
supine within me;
they threaten, they demand.

The question, too, remains:
reflect on their substance,
perish from their beauty,
or extend myself into the void?

Better Times

Better times are needed.
My scalpel is sharp.
More beautiful moments —
longer or shorter or thinner,
just as you please.
The risk of complications is small,
and there are no side effects.
Perfect beauty,
a perfect moment.
All it takes
is my skill as a surgeon
and a local anaesthetic.
It's ambulant;
you'll be out in a day —
minor medical surgery.
And all will be better;
trust me.
A sterile operating table;
forceps and swabs;
bandages
for better times,
more beautiful moments.
Longer or shorter or thinner,
just as you please.

Blissful Oblivion

Your beauty faded

in the cream and saffron lights
of the China tree against your wall.

Shall we kiss, yet?
All in the fullness of time. I told you so.

Autumn's leaves trace windy steps
rustling, whistling, oh so fast.

Your beauty: whitewashed
by daily life.

Glowing May beetles by our side,
we sleepwalk in oblivion.

Where Does

It is official,   the sky is an
exquisite kleptocracy.

We flatter ourselves under it,
                    continuously judging.

We are never obvious,   but always speak
to the underlying similarities
between the judge and the condemned.

          The clouds must dread and abhor the moment,
their burden of the past,
their fear of the future.

They are mutations of chance by a rugged mathematics.
Hear them bang the gavel!

Don't you tell me
              to be naked out and naked in!
Don't you request to
           tear asunder the ties,
           stop over-defining myself!

Don't you
make mention of the splendour of decay, laughing!

We're all just here for a presence,

for anonymous attention.

Where, then, does the end of me
             become the beginning of you?
To pose that question is to answer it.

Time Out of Mind

Two coins in a goldfish pond
Are twins to stars in evening skies.
The moon has blessed our web-spun bond,
We kiss each other in disguise.

We do not know where we belong;
Fleeting memories fill these swooning days;
And city parrots sing their song
To us, silver shooting stars ablaze.

The Visual Linguist

or

Waiting

Forced to leave the endless almond orchards,
forced to leave the sparkling city lights …
What is the shape of this world, of all things indeed?
Whatever the limits of our heads prescribe,

whatever our words can imagine to believe.
What is the shape of this world?
Back in the land of superficial rain,
back in the land of the light that leaves no secrets …

It is no longer round, this world;
we're waiting for a Paradigm Shift,[9]
forced to leave the fragrant harbour,
back in the land of no excuses.

One of these days you might show me
the shape of this world;
what you and I
are made of.

The Emperor and His Clothes

The emperor
is a
middleman in no man's land.

He holds a
sieve.
Importantly, with holes.

What keeps him warm
is the
air between the layers, nothingness:

These little accidents of pleasure
on the
daydream horizon foreclose the cold.

His embroidered suit of armour
is so
light and translucent, threadbare,

that one can see his skin
through
it.

Killing a Man

You in your youth ...
unimaginable!

Jealous

is what I am —
of the sky that looked upon you then,

the wind
that caressed your skin,

the water
that nourished you.

I know you *now*,
which is almost the same
as you then.

But not quite.

It's the not quites that
kill a man.

Imago

Look
Look

Look at me!
Cast your glance
catch my eye
hold my gaze!

Peek or stare or
catch
catch
catch a glimpse!

View me
Watch me
See me!
See — now you grow
test your ego
plant your self!

Sow a seed
for more
more of you!

Behold!

I Sat Down Today

I sat down today
to write a poem,
about your gentle hand
and the grass between us.
But the words I choose
take me prisoner:
too saturated,
semantically bleached,
their meaning
always eludes me.
Ultimately,
whichever rhythm I choose
does not resonate
with what I know.
My heart is filled with waves
that must
displace the quiet waters of a poem.
I sat down today
to write a poem,
but my words do not suffice:
my rhythm is off the beat
because
when our hearts are filled with oceans,
little song is left to sing
and
fewer words are left to say.

Consolation in Windows

When this old friend,
heaviness, plants her fog into
my chest again and nausea
visits me anew to make my
limbs as numb as wood
and desire rears up to replace

this unfathomable pain in me
with real and felt anguish,
when thoughts and memories
turn to a congealed oblivion
and the now seems unendurable,

when future crumbles into black
nothingness and this unknown 'I'
fractures, breaks —
then

one should look out of a window
and find consolation
in the strange fact
that everything else
is still intact.

The Toecutter

We see how the drowsing harbour sinks its mist in
            morning gold
and how shipyard workers smell of salt and rusty nail.
Fishermen's wives gut through another day's produce,
            while
blue-green algae sprawl on ship bows and on granite
            block.

The Toecutter is in town. He hastens, head down,
hands in pockets, his arms exposing kaleidoscopic
            totems
of a tattooed glory. He has opened the box. The box of
            boxes.
The box nobody dared unbolt before. Its lid a weary
            load,

still in his hands as words once spoken now seek him
like a shoal of spectres. He halts, rests his finger and
closes it again, an act little more than wishful thinking.
He hastens, head down, hands in his pockets, along a
            littered street.

And he enters the house, *her* house, takes the lift and
            watches
numbers light up in their ascension; 14 … 15 … 16 …
He looks at the floor, at the ceiling; he stands stock still
and yet is always moving. He is a raging child, barely
            contained.

Of Symbols Misused

His body, rigid as a puppet, jerks toward her room.
He is on his way to surrender to his Old Lady. She almost
comforts, almost loves. He cannot get enough of her or his own
hope. He will see her again and count her amongst his wounded.

'Poetry, or *creativity* like this has a short half life,' he mutters in a tone
inhuman. Leaving the house he smiles like an old and flatulent
summer pond, more sunned upon than sunning. His Old Lady? She is
an echo and a buttress of his identity; an abstraction. The toe fell.

It was an accident, or so they say. He leaves, meanders, becoming
snagged among the barbs of one thought, getting lost in the
loops of the next. He is pained, we know it. The box pins him to
the ground, a wish to sail pricks him like an etherized needle.

He hastens again, head down, hands deep in his pockets.
The box weighs heavy in his trousers, stashed. The skin on his forearm
ripples like a purse of rolling marbles in a sagging bag of leather.
The toe?
It holds all human vanity. There can never be delicacy in repression.

Of Symbols Misused

The Toecutter, whose sharp intellect is captive to fleeting
      impressions,
cuts expressions, wields a willful wit. His compass is his
      enemy.
The box is his life's prime vessel. He'll hand it over, in
      barrels of mirth,
to those shipyard workers where he reigns triumphant,

or pack it in with the old fish guts of venom and
      acrimony.
To set such a soul, drunk with stasis and seduced by
      travel,
on the seas … That is a course and call, for creativity,
a short half life, and a toe severed.

The Snowberry in Me

Barren the stalk, the air is clear —
delicate and small, yet dangles the berry,
beguiled. Ice-cold fragrance hugs
a jam-packed silver void.

Silken, fragile, the berry's sheer skin —
both taut and tender in my mind,
bounds a baleful, inward tug —
the pull of netherwordly time.

Vitreous roots swallow the light,
leaves, ironclad, shimmer and glisten,
the calyx, leaf fibres, close-packed and lucent:

this phlegmatic solitude defines the *I*.
Your love is my frost.
I carry your winter within me.

Narrow

Sick for longing,
homesick for the past;

happy with little,
wanted so much.

What is it?

Do you own
a narrow heart
or throat

that you
cannot
see?

Contemplations

I dissect frogs pinned to a wooden frame;
draw pictures with their blood.
I fight epic battles against Romans
and try on their sandals.
Though foremost, I recite pi:
3.141592653589 ...
I swim in oceans filled with sharks,
kill the biggest sabre-toothed tiger,
denounce all dogmas and doctrines,
and free ten prisoners of war.
I write volumes of cheap romance,
defiantly walk on pavement cracks,
dodge treacherous quicksand, and
re-sound throw-away comments a million-fold.
Occasionally, I compose symphonies and
re-live cheap old memories of
that woman who once caressed my hair.
I make good what once I regretted
and kick all liars in their shins.

Then, there is always my stop
and it is time for me to get off the bus.

Northern Lights

'Never mind,' you said
(and your hat slipped
over your brow),
'The peaceful dove'
(your eyes
scraped the ground),
'That I saw in the sky
was, in fact,
an old plastic bag'.

Many years ago, you were
sharply passioned;
but now regret has
washed you out,
and every third thought
is your own distress.
You're hungry. You
hold your nose high
to sniff the music of

the occasion that plays you.
Let indulgence judge.
Let us carve little men
from bananas. —
Better people
than you and I. —
Let us take the money
and seek the Northern
Lights.

Mind Matters

The truth: we are anxious.
The brutal baleful beasts are prowling —
with boundaries of flesh and circumstance —
their thousand fingers hot and brittle,
grabbing, grabbing, grabbing in perpetuity.

We fear these monsters' stifling furs.
Buckling beneath their breath, we seek to bear
their restlessness, survive their never-ending
strains, demands and interpellations;
we shudder as we sense their heft.

Frantically, we tend to them.
With Sudoku, television, music, inane
conversations on mobile phones or punched
into the black teeth of a rotten keyboard
about the weather, or a handbag. —

It's scraps of mind candy
we throw to soothe their throats. — We feel
they momentarily desist. Exhaling then, we brace
ourselves for the returning fear: the brutes
may one day feast on our uneasy minds,

that is
autophagise.

Of Symbols Misused: Advance Responses

Newton's first collection is bold, eclectic and tightly crafted. She is attentive both to the delicate nuances of solitude and to the brash declarations with which we sometimes disguise ourselves. The collection echoes with a resounding delight in words: images are fresh, sometimes strikingly memorable and often powered by an edgy energy which compels the reader to do that wonderful thing: inhabit the poetry. – Martin Alexander, author of *Clearing Ground* and Poetry Editor of the *Asia Literary Review*.

Mary-Jane Newton's first collection displays boldness of spirit and a buccaneering sense of adventure in its forays with language, matched by energy, a wry sense of humour and humility in the light of the poet's responsibilities, thus making it a joy to read, at turns sensuous and arch in tones and angles. – Peter Carpenter, author of *After the Goldrush* and other published works and Chair of the Poetry Society, United Kingdom.

Mary-Jane Newton's poetry is so unexpected it often startles me. A charged, radically honest book with zest and panache; she tells it like it is, with wit and a touch of irony. Her voice is as unique as her approach to the poems. And, as always, her honesty is refreshing and uniquely personal. It is, simply, poetry you will find nowhere else. – Geoffrey Gatza, Editor at BlazeVOX [books] and author of numerous collections of poetry.

Mary Jane Newton's poetry is quicksilver! Its shifts are often rapid and at times deceptively breezy. But don't be deceived: the love poems of this collection (and they are all love poems) are incisive, surprising and revelatory. As a poet Newton is unflinching and honest, and her words offer insight always at the expense of safety. – Michael Holland, author of *Metaflora*.

These are love poems, poems of leave-taking and of sudden illumination. The writing, always beautifully executed, emerges from a polyphonic imagination. – Eddie Tay, author of *The Mental Life of Cities* and Reviews Editor of *Cha: An Asian Literary Journal*.

Notes

[1] Burke, K. (1966). *Language As Symbolic Action*. Berkley & Los Angeles: University of California Press, p. 16. For Burke, human behaviour is most difficult and problematic in those instances in which symbols use human beings, rather than human beings use symbols.

[2] Peter Weiss (1916–1982) was an acclaimed German writer, painter and artist, arguably most famous for his play *Marat/Sade*, a play that, in part, explores issues around sadism, i.e. power, pleasure and pain. Peter Weiss was also the name of my father, while "Albert Blades" was the pseudonym he used in the unpublished writings he shared with his family. Thematic similarities in their writings link these two manifestations of Peter Weiss.

[3] Harry Houdini: Hungarian-American magician, escapologist and stunt performer.

[4] After a book of the same title by Ernest Becker.

[5] Conrad Moffat Black, Baron Black of Crossharbour, is a newspaper magnate convicted of criminal fraud.

[6] Compare Sigmund Freud's theories on dreams, most notably *Die Traumdeutung*.

[7] It is a common misperception that the word 'nylon' is a blend of the words 'New York' and 'London'. Though etymologically, the word was developed from 'No run' the provisional name this fabric was given by its makers.

[8] This poem is loosely based on an Egyptian creation myth.

[9] Compare Thomas Kuhn's *The Structure of Scientific Revolutions* (1962), in which Kuhn coins the term 'paradigm shift' to denote a complete re-understanding of fundamental assumptions in science.

Smoked Pearl by Akin Jeje
To Eastern Lands by Roger Uren
Unlocking by Mary-Jane Newton
Violet by Carolina Ilica
Wonder, Lust & Itchy Feet by Sally Dellow
The Year of the Apparitions by José Manuel Sevilla

INTERNATIONAL PROVERSE POETRY PRIZE ANTHOLOGIES

Mingled Voices ed Gillian and Verner Bickley
Mingled Voices 2 ed Gillian and Verner Bickley
Mingled Voices 3 ed Gillian and Verner Bickley

POETRY IN CHINESE

Moving House and Other Poems by Gillian Bickley (in Chinese with additional contents & b/w photographs)

EDUCATIONAL
(English Language)

Poems to Enjoy, Book 1 by Verner Bickley (3rd Ed) w. 1 audio CD (Graded poetry anthology w. teaching and learning notes, glossary, etc.)
Poems to Enjoy, Book 2 by Verner Bickley (3rd Ed) w. 2 audio CDs (Graded poetry anthology w. teaching and learning notes, glossary, etc.)
Poems to Enjoy, Book 3 by Verner Bickley (3rd Ed) w. 2 audio CDs (Graded poetry anthology w. teaching and learning notes, glossary, etc.)
Poems to Enjoy, Book 4 by Verner Bickley (3rd Ed) w. 2 audio CDs (Graded poetry anthology w. teaching and learning notes, glossary, etc.)
Poems to Enjoy, Book 5 by Verner Bickley (3rd Ed) w. 3 audio CDs (Graded poetry anthology w. teaching and learning notes, glossary, etc.)